ARTIST TRANSCRIPTIONS PIANO

The Vince Guaraldi COLLECTION

Photo courtesy of Fantasy, Inc.

ISBN 978-0-634-03099-4

HAL•LEONARD® CORPORATION

7777 W. BLUEMOUND RD. P.O. BOX 13819 MILWAUKEE, WI 53213

For all works contained herein:
Unauthorized copying, arranging, adapting, recording or public performance is an infringement of copyright.
Infringers are liable under the law.

Visit Hal Leonard Online at
www.halleonard.com

The Vince Guaraldi
COLLECTION

CONTENTS

BIOGRAPHY

Vince Guaraldi called himself a "reformed boogie-woogie piano player." Of course, he was much more than that. In his all-too-short forty-seven year life, he won a Grammy Award for his recording of "Cast Your Fate to the Wind," and created music for the Peanuts television specials that have assured his place as one of the most beloved composers in the jazz world.

Born in San Francisco in 1928, his earliest influences were Jimmy Yancey, Albert Ammons and Pete Johnson. After attending San Francisco State College and serving in the military, Guaraldi returned to San Francisco to continue making music. He free-lanced in the '50s, performing with the Bill Harris - Chubby Jackson band, Georgie Auld, Woody Herman and Sonny Criss. He recorded with Stan Getz in 1957, and scored a major triumph at the first Monterey Jazz Festival in 1958 as pianist with Cal Tjader's latin band.

In 1962, he recorded an album called *Jazz Impressions of Black Orpheus*, inspired by the soundtrack to the hit motion picture. "Samba de Orfeu" and "Cast Your Fate to the Wind" were issued as singleS and "Cast Your Fate" was played frequently on the radio, even though it was the B-side of the single. The album went on to sell almost 500,000 copies.

By the mid '60s, Guaraldi continued to play with his trio, and toured and recorded with Brazilian guitarist Bola Sete. On the advice of writer Ralph J. Gleason, Guaraldi was hired by producer Lee Mendelson to write themes for a documentary on Charles Schulz, the creator of the comic strip, "Peanuts," and a soundtrack album of Guaraldi's themes was released. While the documentary didn't sell, the album did, and the themes were later re-worked for the animated "Peanuts" television specials. Guaraldi would score fifteen network "Peanuts" cartoon specials.

In 1965, Guaraldi played a concert at San Francisco's Grace Cathedral, featuring his trio and a mixed chorus performing his sacred music, preceding Duke Ellington's sacred concert there by four months. He continued performing and composing, even performing with the Grateful Dead, until he suffered a heart attack in 1976.

DISCOGRAPHY

Cast Your Fate to the Wind,
Manha de Carnaval,
Samba de Orfeu –
4/18/62 – LP: Fantasy 8089;
CD: OJCCD-437

Christmas Time Is Here,
Greensleeves, O Tannenbaum –
1965 – LP: Fantasy 8431 (+CD)
(Greensleeves appears
on the CD only)

Outra Vez –
12/4/62 –
LP: Fantasy 8352;
CD: OJCCD-951

Linus and Lucy –
1964 –
LP: Fantasy 8430 (+CD)

Star Song – 1963 –
LP: Fantasy 8356;
CD: FCD-24756

Cast Your Fate to the Wind

Words and Music by Vince Guaraldi and Carel Werver

Copyright © 1961 by Atzal Music, Inc.
Copyright Renewed
All Rights Administered by Unichappell Music Inc.
International Copyright Secured   All Rights Reserved

Laid Back

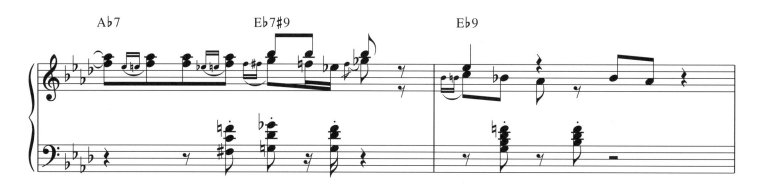

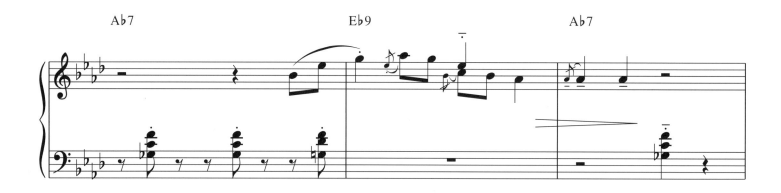

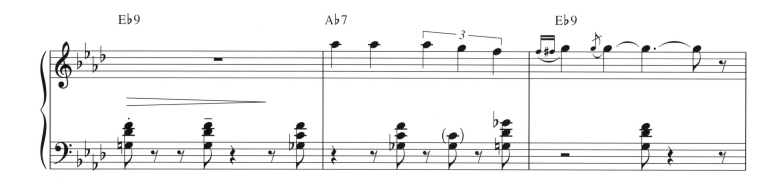

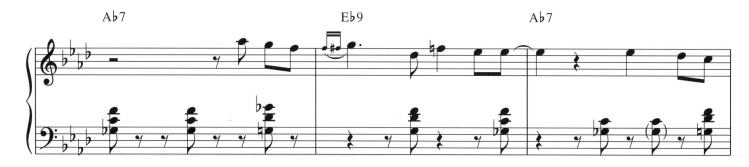

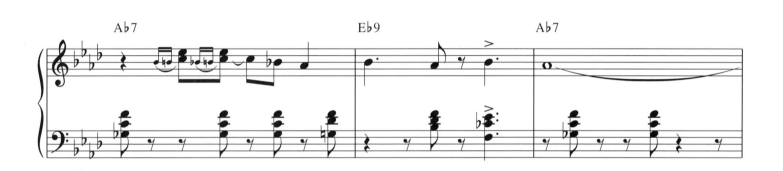

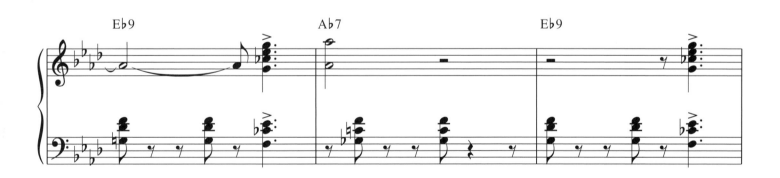

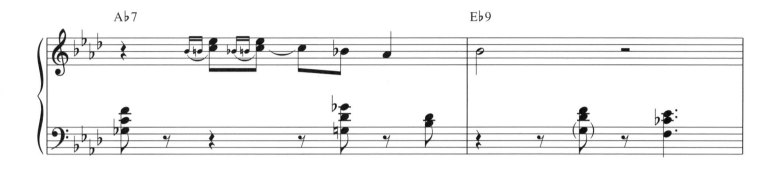

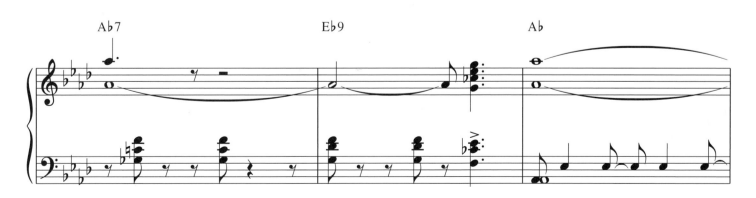

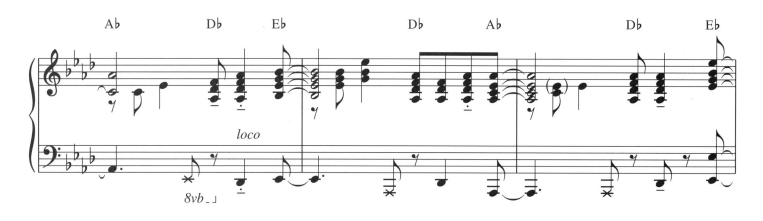

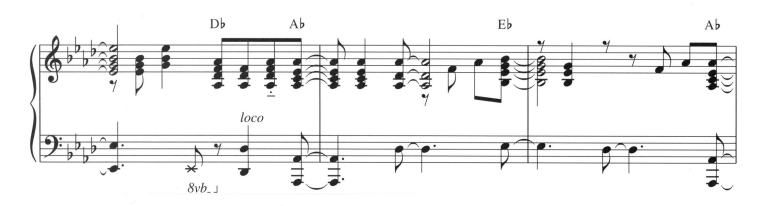

Christmas Time Is Here

Words by Lee Mendelson
Music by Vince Guaraldi

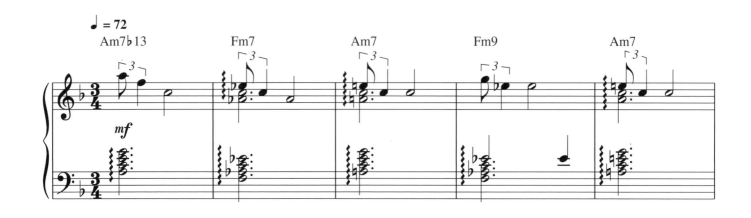

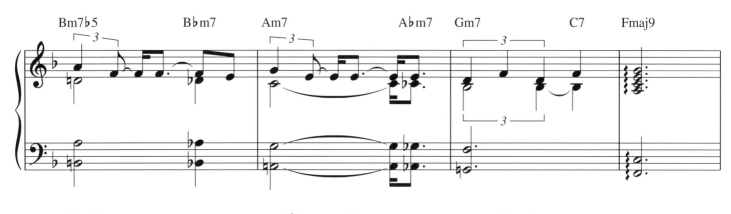

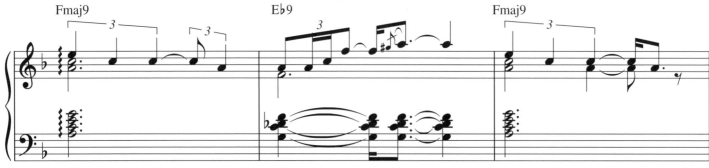

Copyright © 1966 LEE MENDELSON FILM PRODUCTIONS, INC.
Copyright Renewed
International Copyright Secured   All Rights Reserved

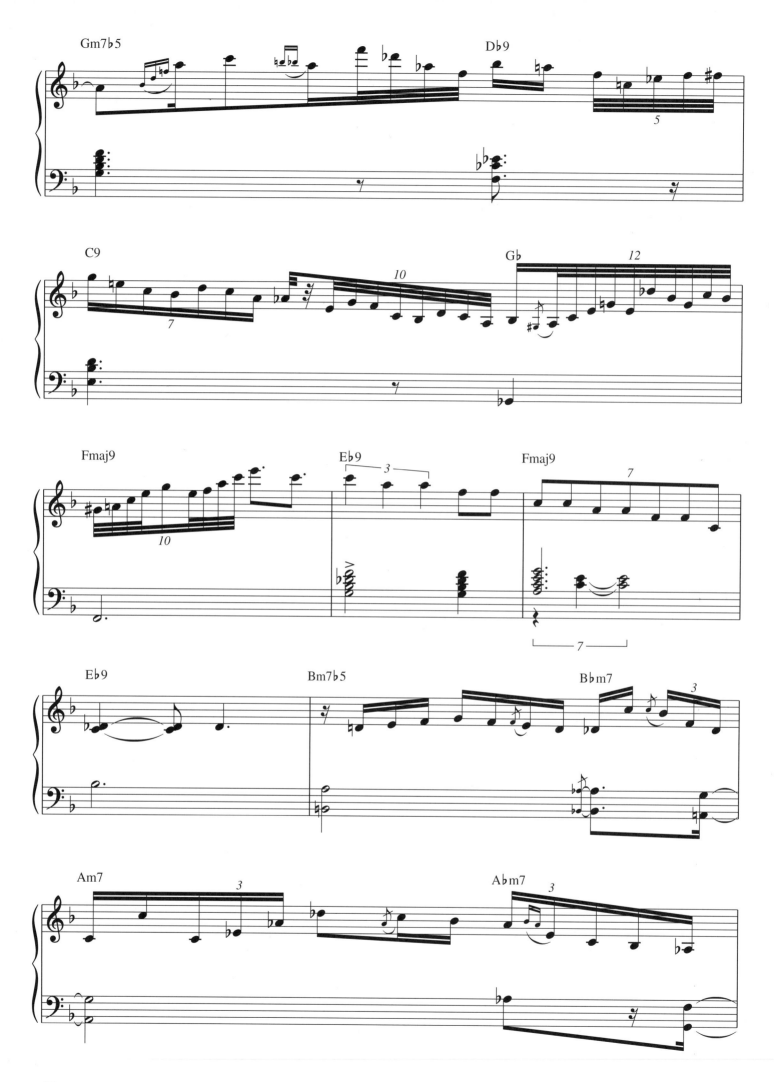

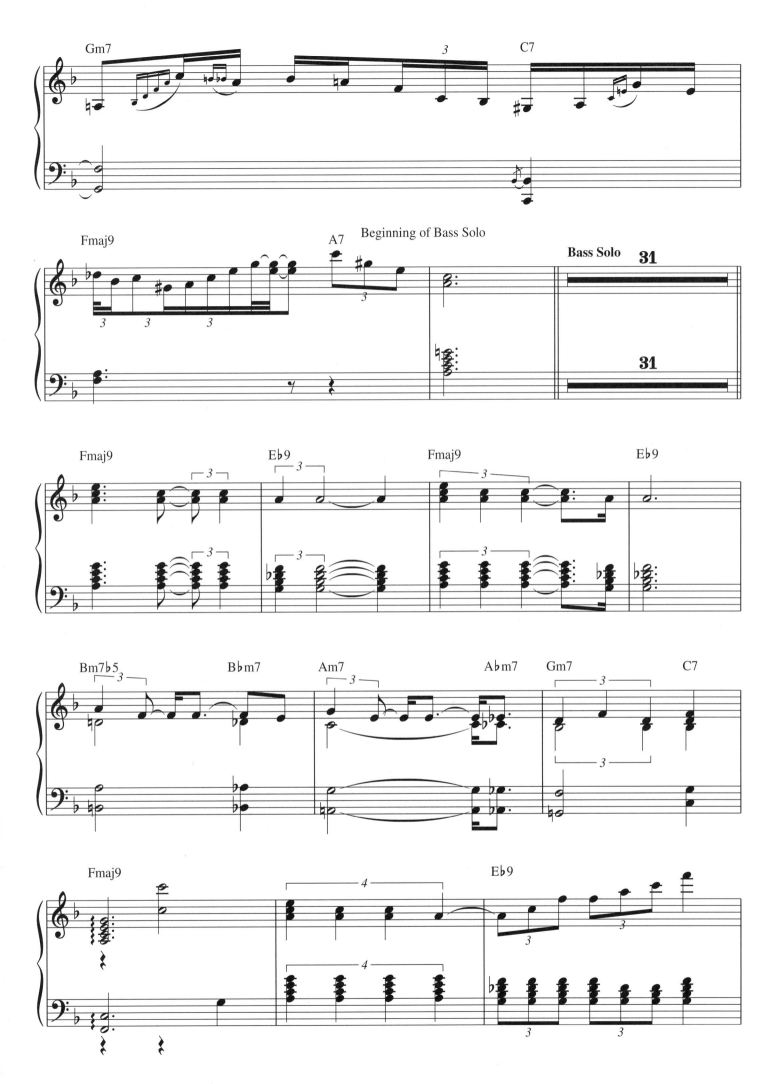

Linus and Lucy

By Vince Guaraldi

Copyright © 1965 LEE MENDELSON FILM PRODUCTIONS, INC.
Copyright Renewed
International Copyright Secured   All Rights Reserved

Manha De Carnaval
(A Day in the Life of a Fool)
Words by Carl Sigman
Music by Luiz Bonfa

Copyright © 1966 by Les Nouvelles Editions Meridian
Copyright Renewed
All Rights Administered by Chappell & Co.
International Copyright Secured   All Rights Reserved

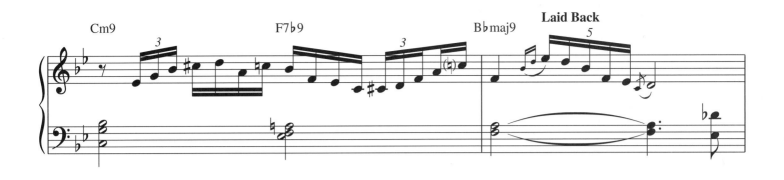

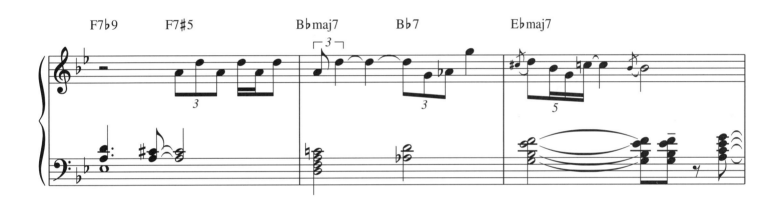

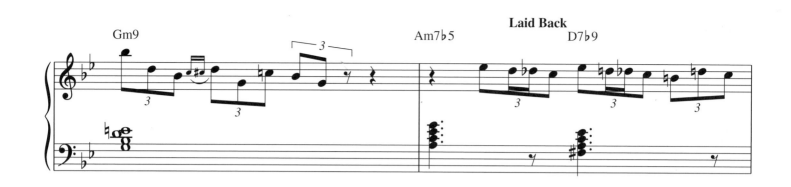

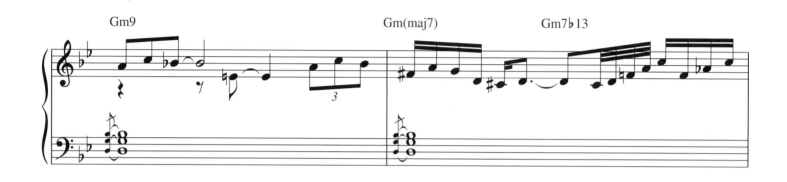

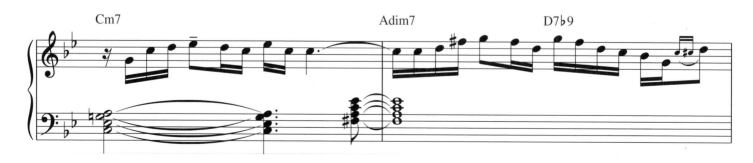

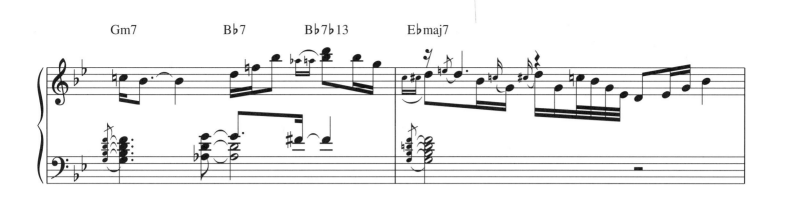

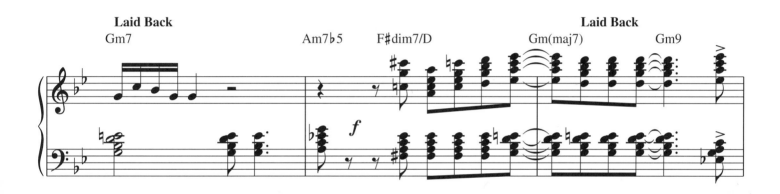

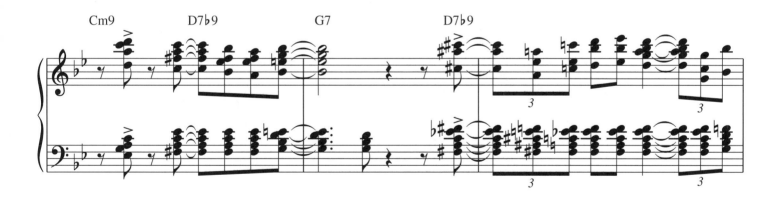

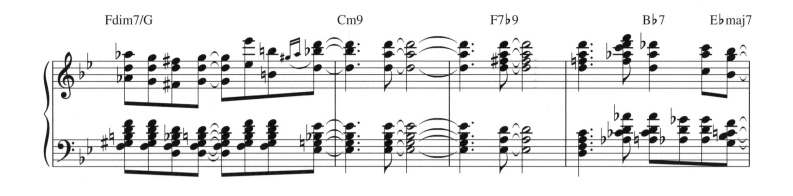

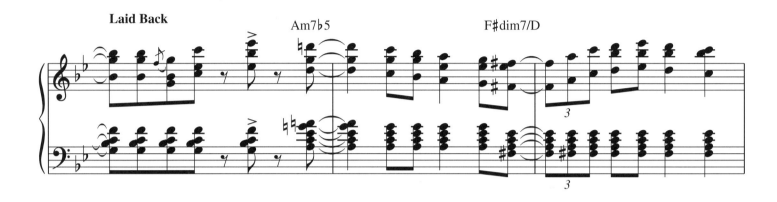

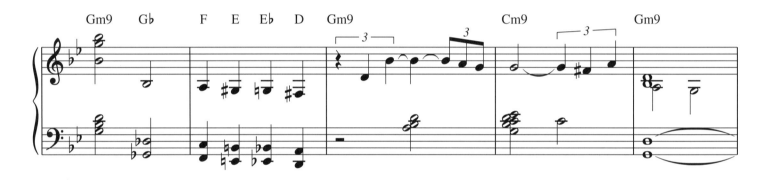

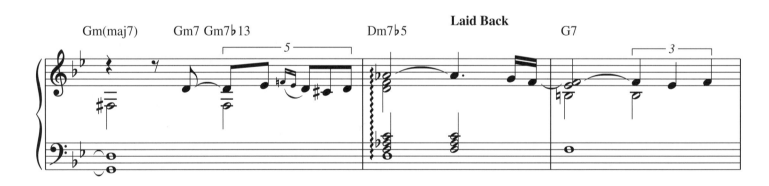

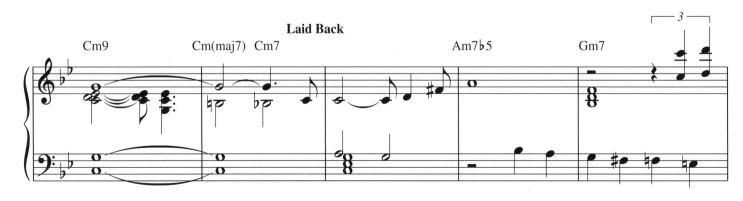

O Tannenbaum

Traditional
Arranged by Vince Guaraldi

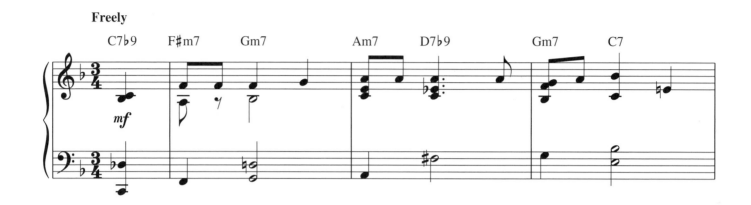

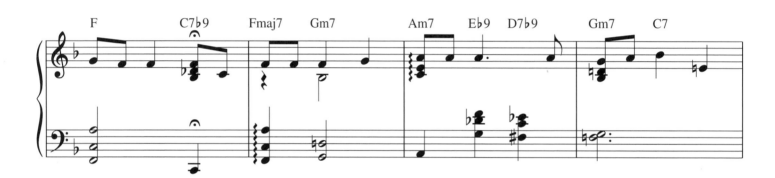

Copyright © 1966 LEE MENDELSON FILM PRODUCTIONS, INC.
Copyright Renewed
International Copyright Secured   All Rights Reserved

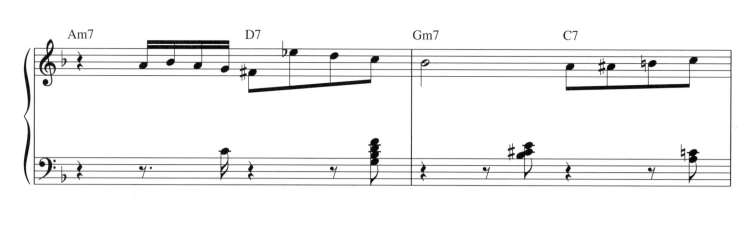

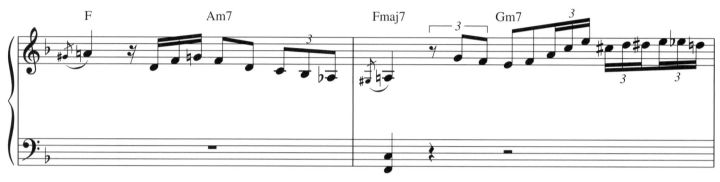

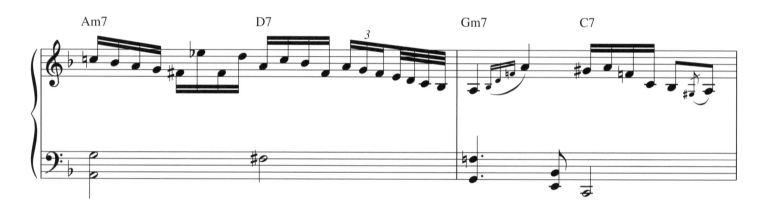

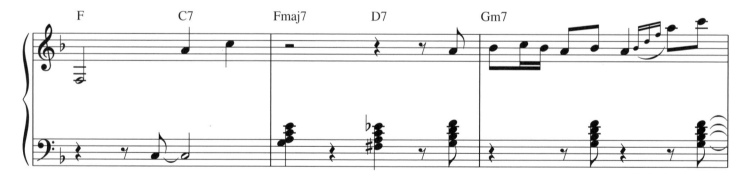

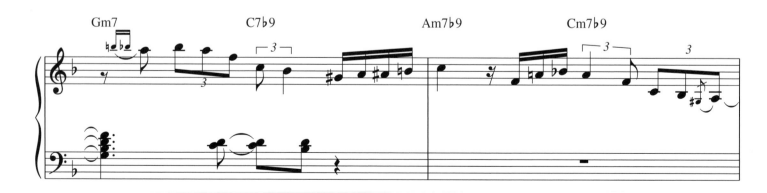

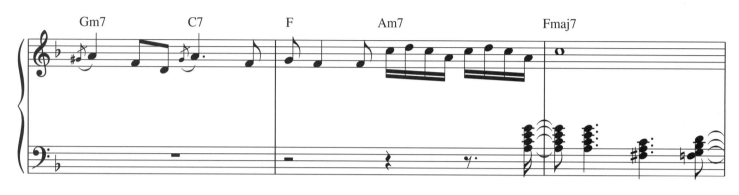

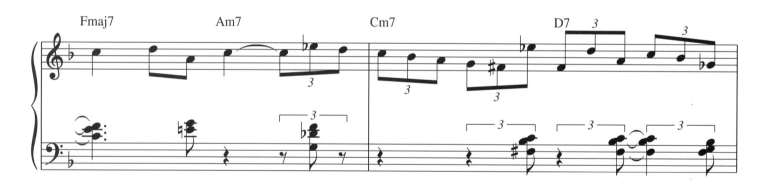

Greensleeves

Traditional
Arranged by Vince Guaraldi

Copyright © 1965 LEE MENDELSON FILM PRODUCTIONS, INC.
Copyright Renewed
International Copyright Secured   All Rights Reserved

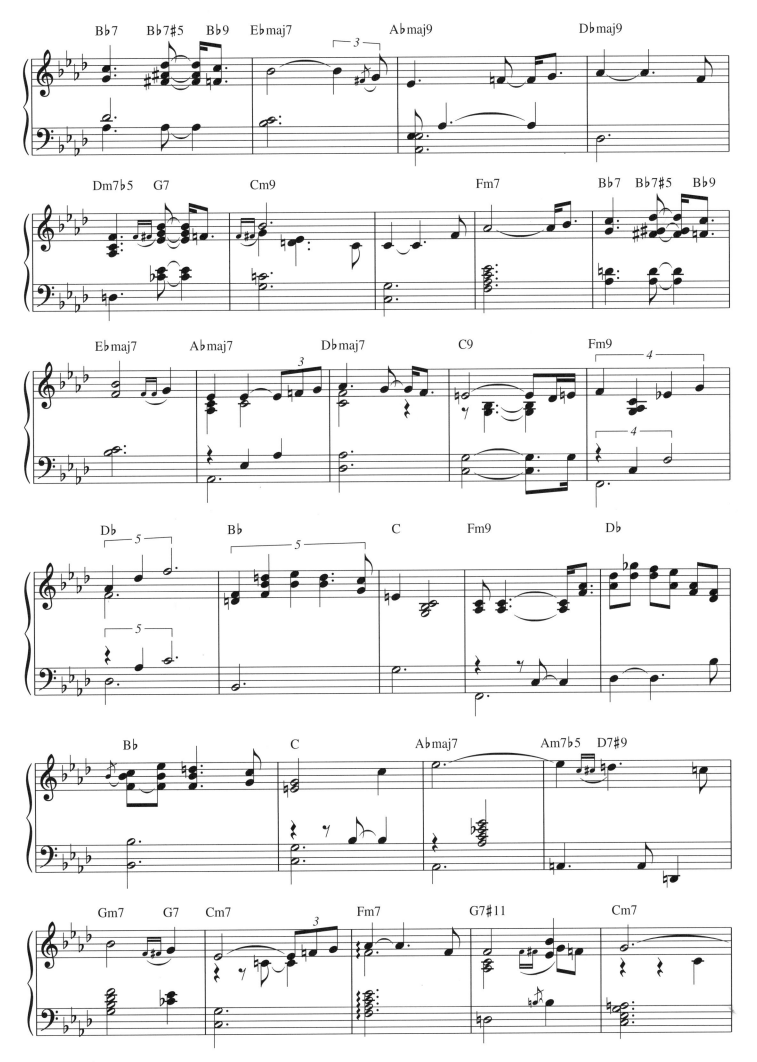

Outra Vez

Words and Music by Antonio Carlos Jobim

Copyright © 1962 Corcovado Music Corp.
Copyright Renewed
International Copyright Secured   All Rights Reserved

Samba De Orfeu

Words by Antonio Maria
Music by Luiz Bonfa

Copyright © 1959 by Nouvelles Editions Meridian
Copyrights for the United States of America and Canada Renewed and Assigned to Chappell & Co. and United Artists Music Co., Inc.
All Rights Administered by Chappell & Co.
International Copyright Secured   All Rights Reserved

Fmaj9　　　　　　　　　F#dim7

Gm7　　　　　　　　Cdim7　　　　　　　　Gm7

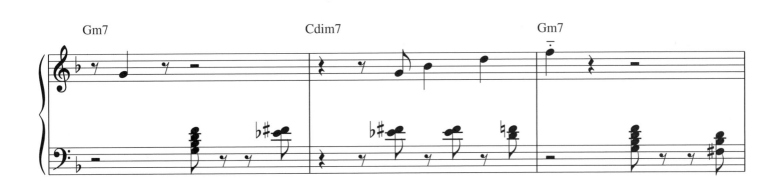

F#+/G　　　　　　　Gm7

C7　　　　　　　　Fmaj7

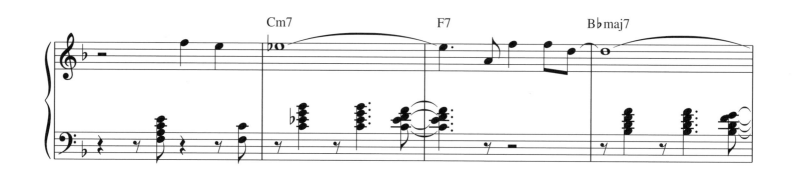

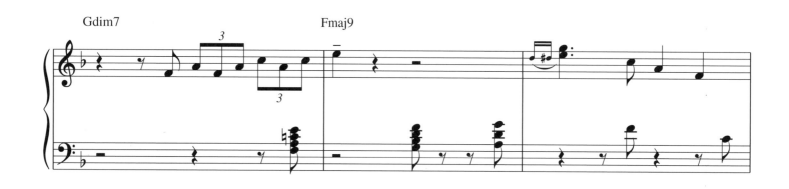

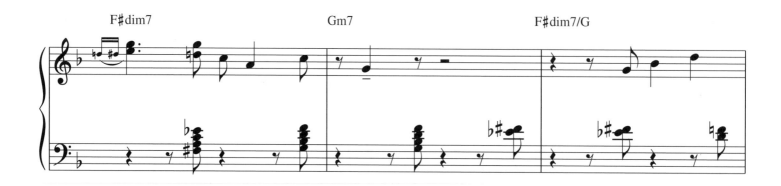

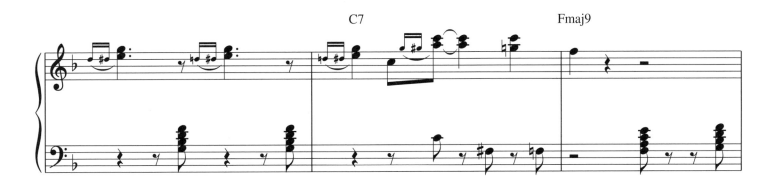

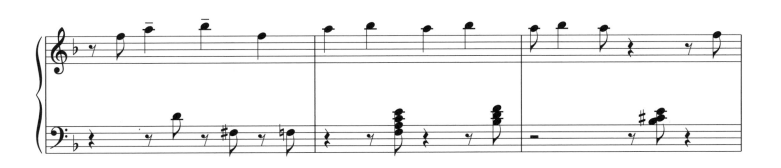

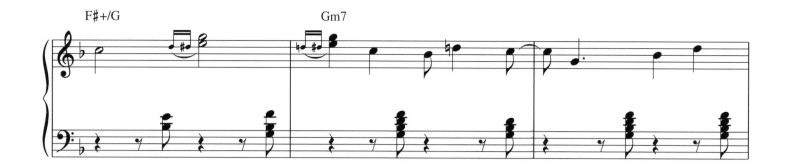

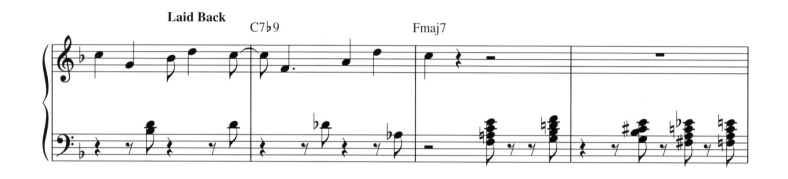

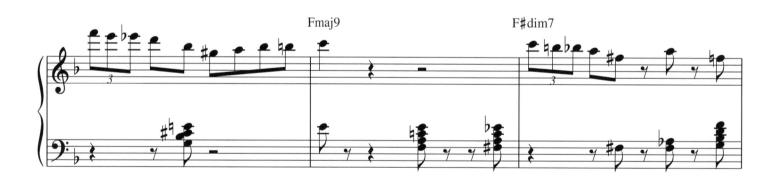

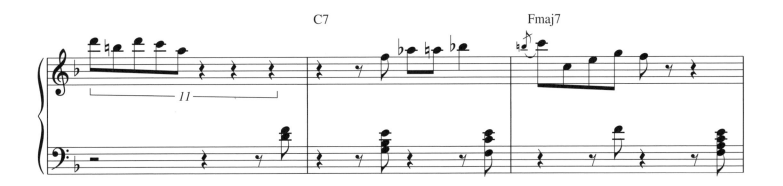

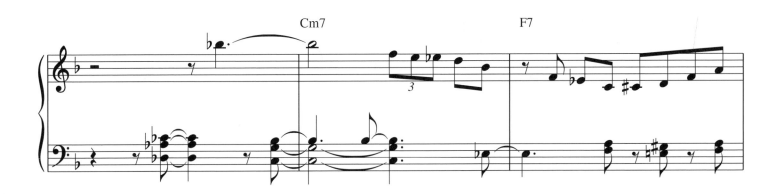

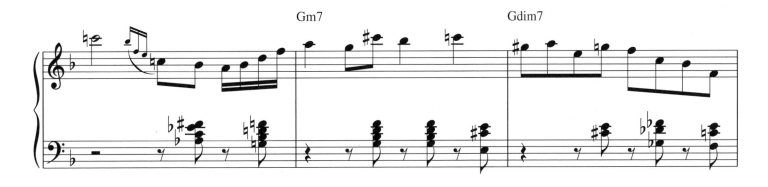

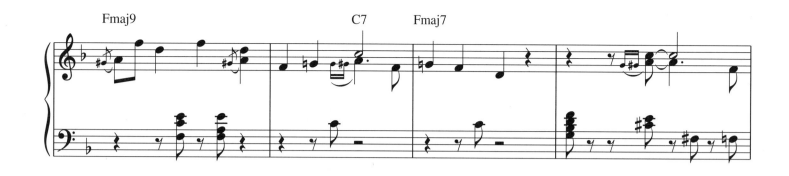

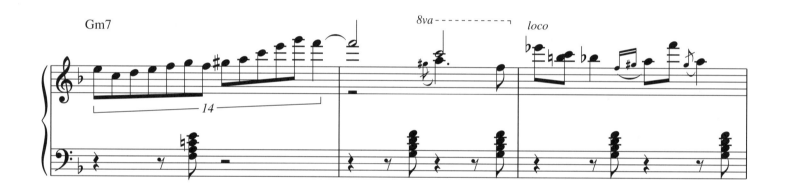

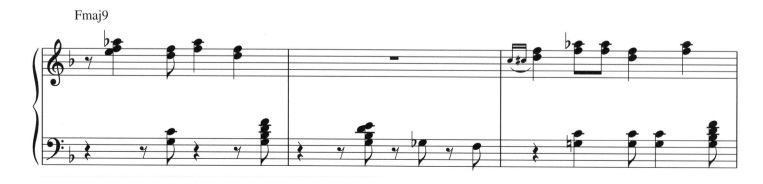

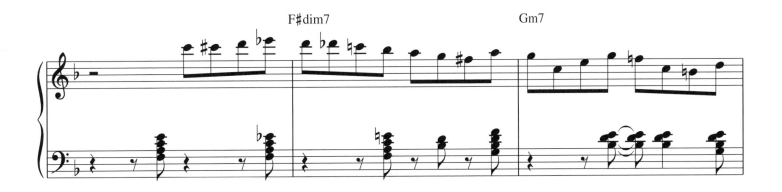

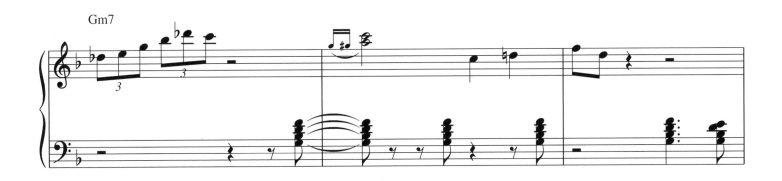

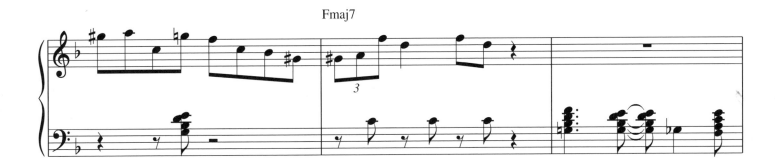

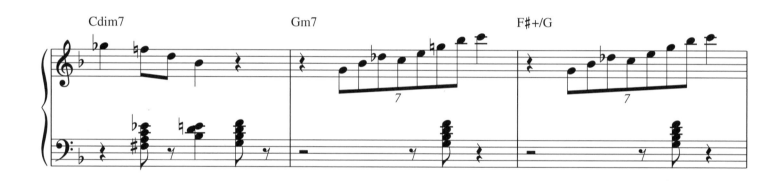

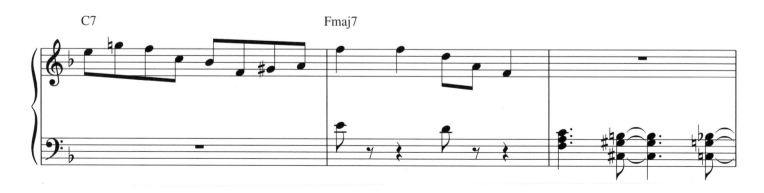

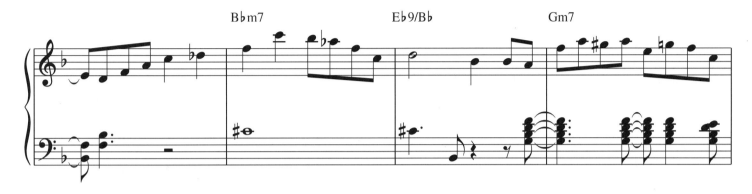

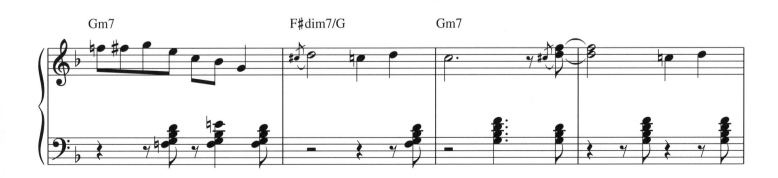

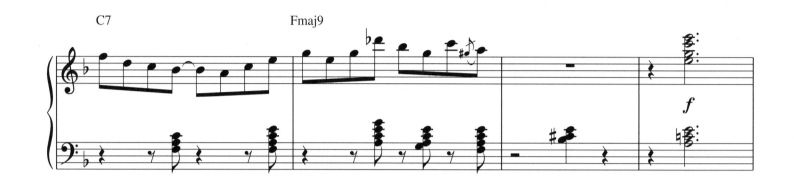

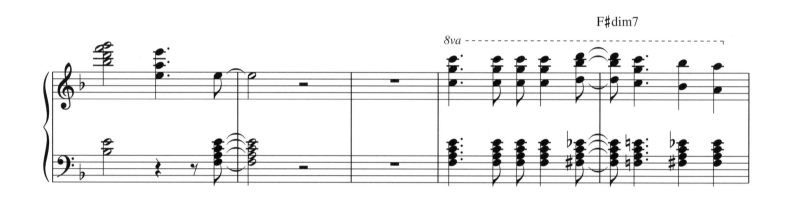

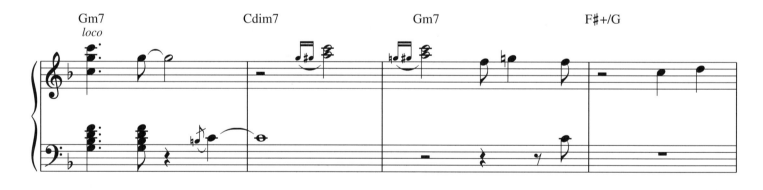

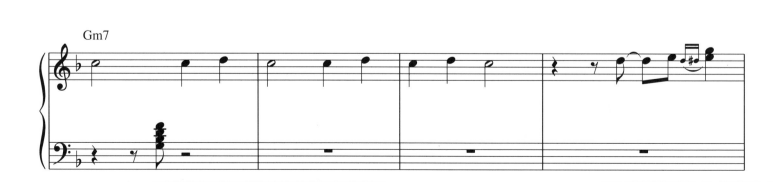

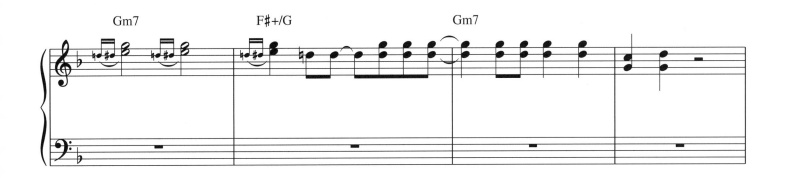

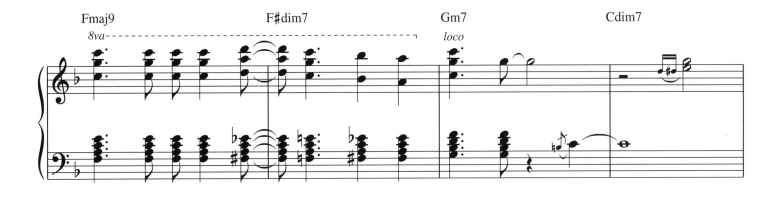

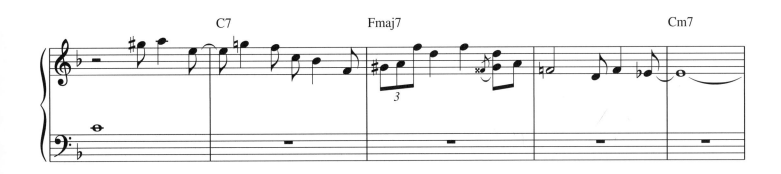

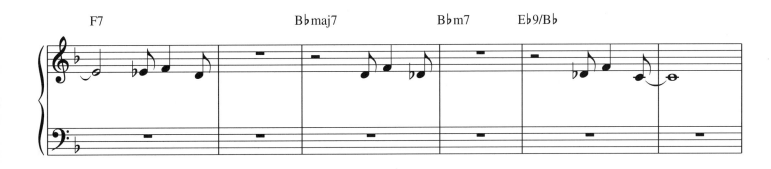

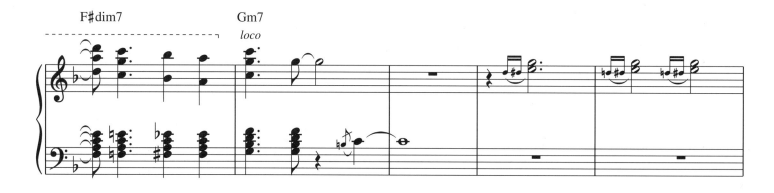

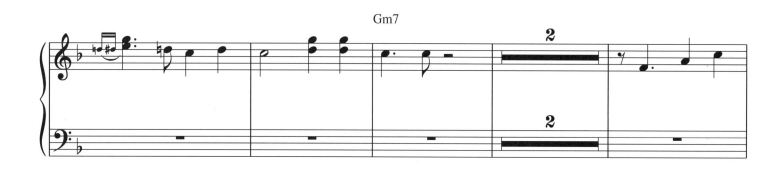

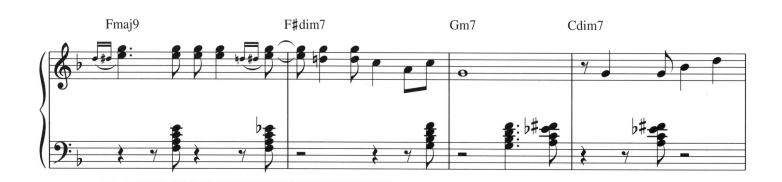

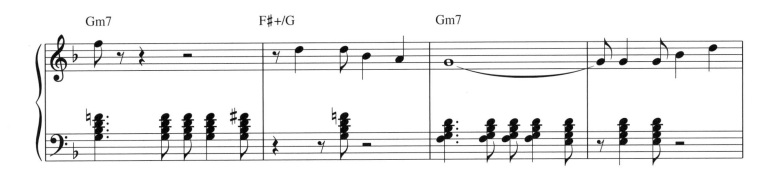

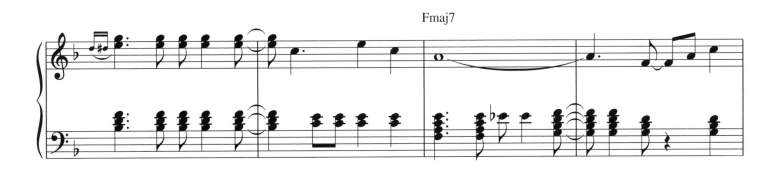

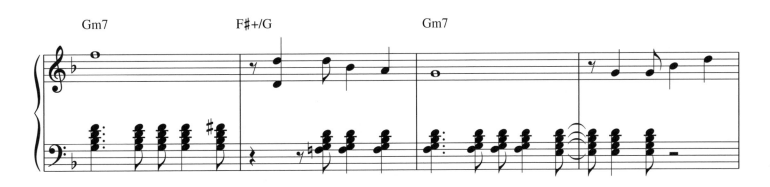

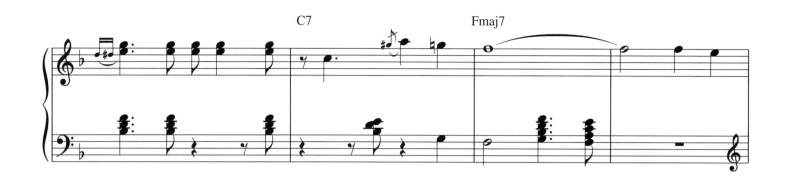

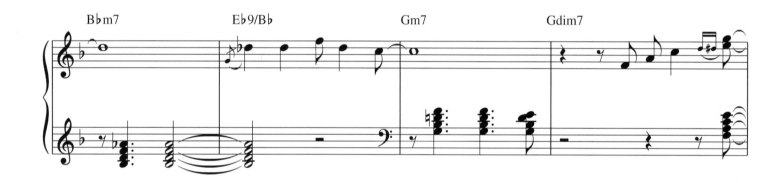

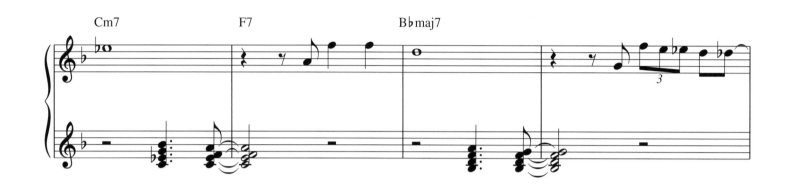

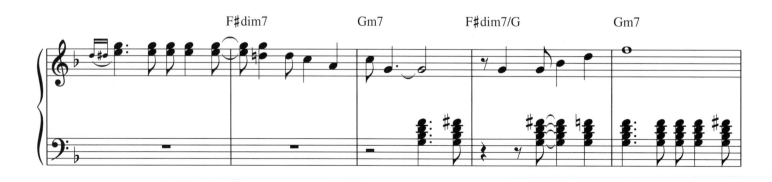

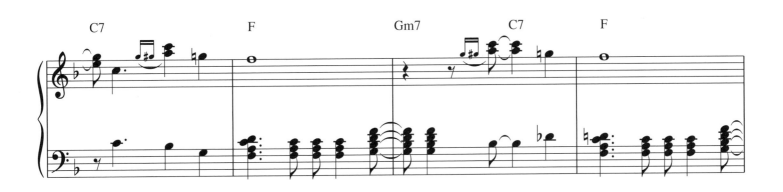

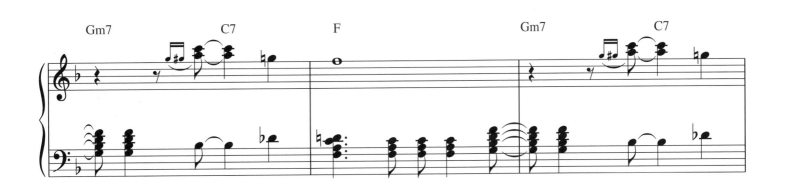

Star Song

By Vince Guaraldi

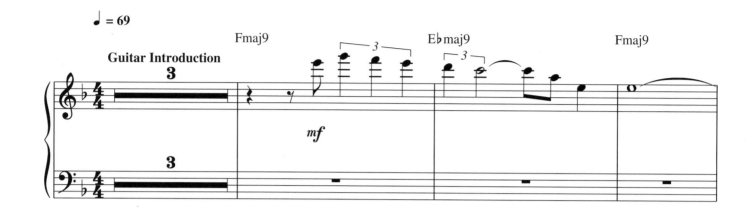

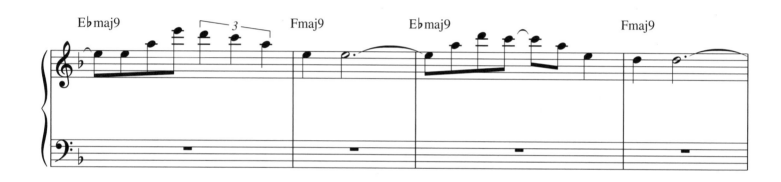

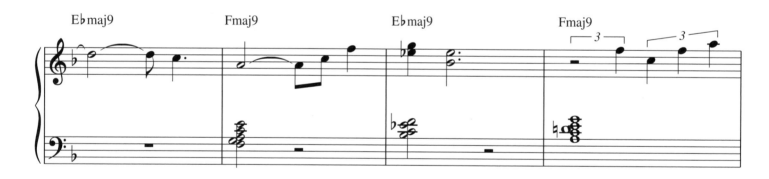

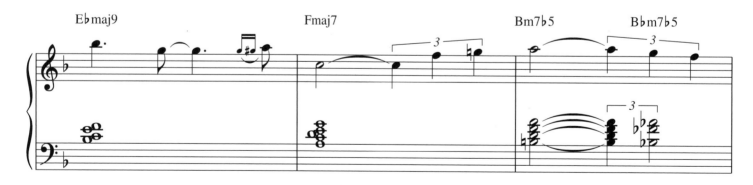

Copyright © 1964 LEE MENDELSON FILM PRODUCTIONS, INC.
Copyright Renewed
International Copyright Secured   All Rights Reserved

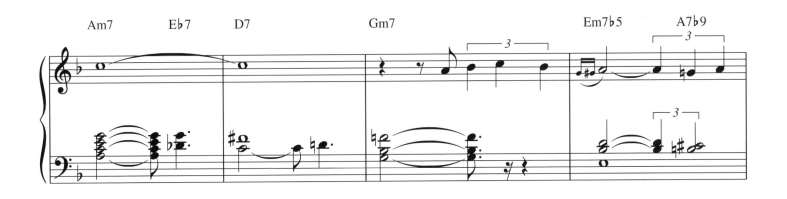

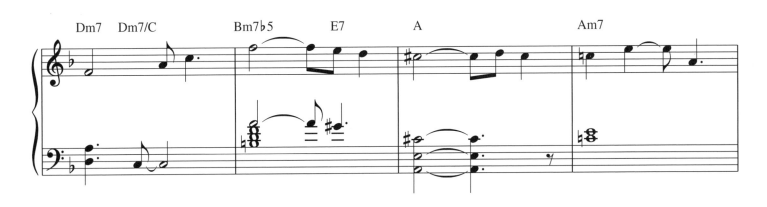

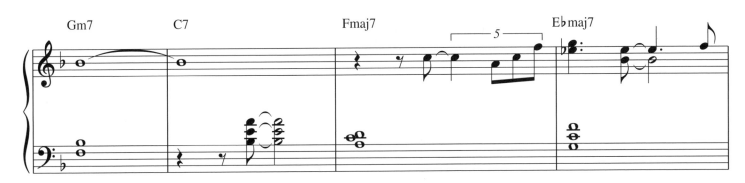

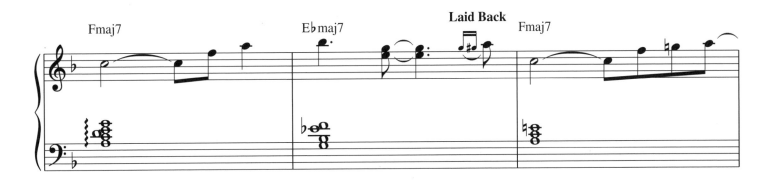

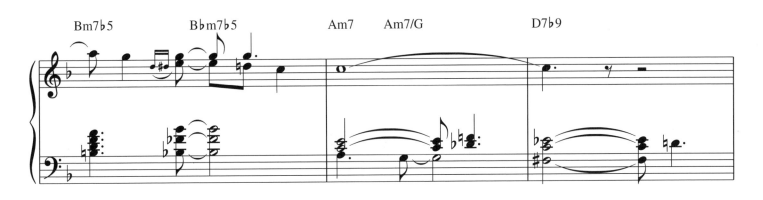

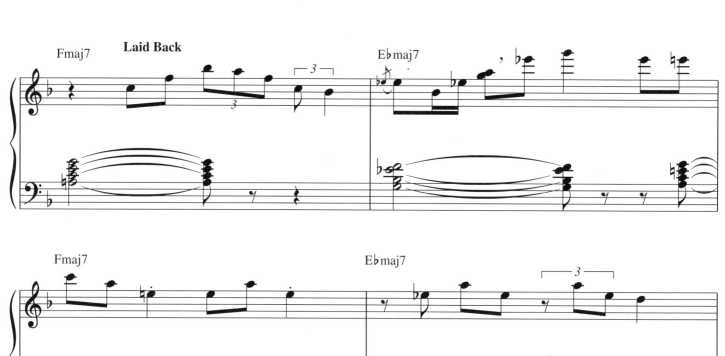

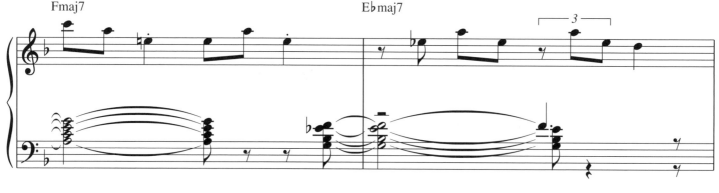

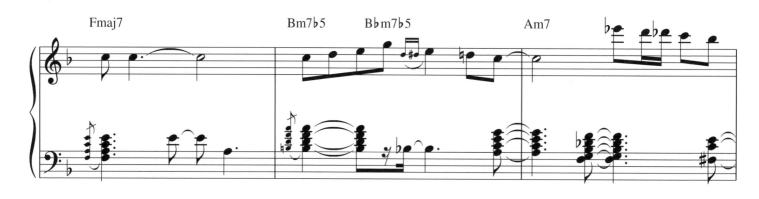

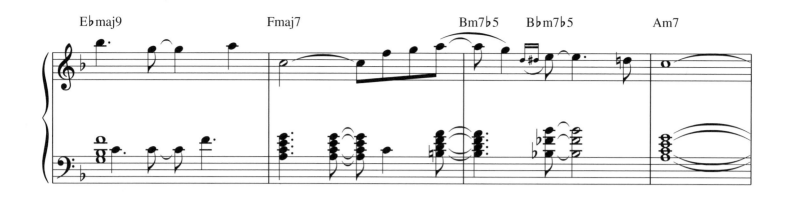

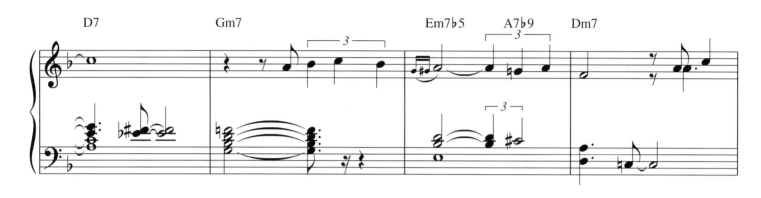

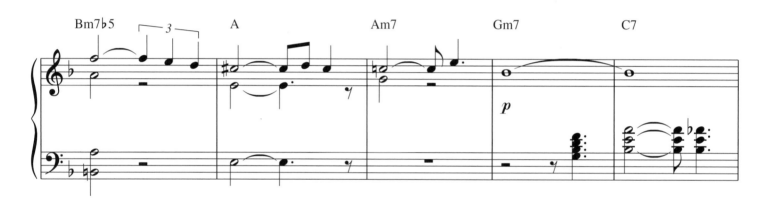

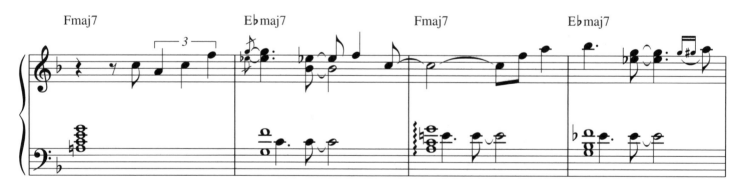

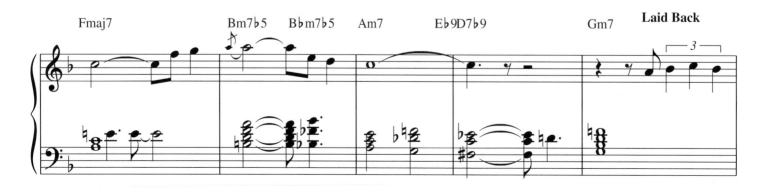

ARTIST TRANSCRIPTIONS®

Artist Transcriptions are authentic, note-for-note transcriptions of today's hottest artists in jazz, pop and rock. These outstanding, accurate arrangements are in an easy-to-read format which includes all essential lines. **Artist Transcriptions** can be used to perform, sequence or for reference.

CLARINET
00672423 Buddy De Franco Collection $19.95

FLUTE
00672379 Eric Dolphy Collection...........................$19.95
00672582 The Very Best of James Galway $16.99
00672372 James Moody Collection –
　　　　　Sax and Flute $19.95

GUITAR & BASS
00660113 The Guitar Style of George Benson.......$16.99
00699072 Guitar Book of Pierre Bensusan $29.95
00672331 Ron Carter – Acoustic Bass..................$19.99
00672573 Ray Brown – Legendary Jazz Bassist ..$19.99
00672307 Stanley Clarke Collection......................$19.99
00660115 Al Di Meola –
　　　　　Friday Night in San Francisco...............$16.99
00604043 Al Di Meola –
　　　　　Music, Words, Pictures $14.95
00672574 Al Di Meola –
　　　　　Pursuit of Radical Rhapsody $22.99
00125617 Best of Herb Ellis $19.99
00673245 Jazz Style of Tal Farlow $19.99
00699306 Jim Hall – Exploring Jazz Guitar...........$19.99
00604049 Allan Holdsworth –
　　　　　Reaching for the Uncommon Chord $17.99
00699215 Leo Kottke – Eight Songs $17.99
00672353 Joe Pass Collection $19.99
00673216 John Patitucci.......................................$17.99
00027083 Django Reinhardt Anthology $16.99
00672374 Johnny Smith Guitar Solos....................$19.99

PIANO & KEYBOARD
00672338 Monty Alexander Collection $19.95
00672487 Monty Alexander Plays Standards $19.95
00672520 Count Basie Collection $19.95
00192307 Bebop Piano Legends............................$19.99
00113680 Blues Piano Legends.............................$19.99
00278003 A Charlie Brown Christmas $17.99
00672439 Cyrus Chestnut Collection $19.95
00672300 Chick Corea – Paint the World..............$16.99
14037739 Storyville Presents Duke Ellington $19.99
00146105 Bill Evans – Alone.................................$17.99
00672537 Bill Evans at Town Hall..........................$19.99
00672548 The Mastery of Bill Evans $16.99
00672425 Bill Evans – Piano Interpretations........$22.99
00672365 Bill Evans – Piano Standards.................$19.99
00121885 Bill Evans – Time Remembered $19.99
00672510 Bill Evans Trio – Vol. 1: 1959-1961 ......$24.95
00672511 Bill Evans Trio – Vol. 2: 1962-1965.......$24.99
00672512 Bill Evans Trio – Vol. 3: 1968-1974.......$24.99
00672513 Bill Evans Trio – Vol. 4: 1979-1980.......$24.95
00672381 Tommy Flanagan Collection $24.99
00193332 Erroll Garner – Concert by the Sea.......$19.99
00672492 Benny Goodman Collection $16.95
00672486 Vince Guaraldi Collection......................$19.99
00672419 Herbie Hancock Collection....................$19.95
00672438 Hampton Hawes $19.95
14037738 Storyville Presents Earl Hines...............$19.99

00672322 Ahmad Jamal Collection $24.99
00255671 Jazz Piano Masterpieces......................$19.99
00124367 Jazz Piano Masters Play
　　　　　Rodgers & Hammerstein $19.99
00672564 Best of Jeff Lorber...............................$17.99
00672476 Brad Mehldau Collection.......................$19.99
00672388 Best of Thelonious Monk $19.95
00672389 Thelonious Monk Collection $22.99
00672390 Thelonious Monk Plays
　　　　　Jazz Standards – Volume 1 ....$19.99
00672391 Thelonious Monk Plays
　　　　　Jazz Standards – Volume 2 ....$19.95
00672433 Jelly Roll Morton – The Piano Rolls $16.99
00672553 Charlie Parker for Piano $19.95
00672542 Oscar Peterson – Jazz Piano Solos.....$17.99
00672562 Oscar Peterson –
　　　　　A Jazz Portrait of Frank Sinatra............$19.95
00264094 Oscar Peterson – Night Train $19.99
00672544 Oscar Peterson – Originals $10.99
00672532 Oscar Peterson – Plays Broadway........$19.95
00672531 Oscar Peterson –
　　　　　Plays Duke Ellington $24.99
00672563 Oscar Peterson –
　　　　　A Royal Wedding Suite $19.99
00672569 Oscar Peterson – Tracks $19.99
00672533 Oscar Peterson – Trios.........................$24.95
00672543 Oscar Peterson Trio –
　　　　　Canadiana Suite $12.99
00672534 Very Best of Oscar Peterson................$22.95
00672371 Bud Powell Classics.............................$19.99
00672376 Bud Powell Collection $19.95
00672507 Gonzalo Rubalcaba Collection $19.95
00672303 Horace Silver Collection........................$22.99
00672316 Art Tatum Collection $24.99
00672355 Art Tatum Solo Book $19.95
00673215 McCoy Tyner $19.99
00672321 Cedar Walton Collection $19.95
00672519 Kenny Werner Collection.......................$19.95
00672434 Teddy Wilson Collection $19.95

SAXOPHONE
00672566 The Mindi Abair Collection $14.99
00673244 Julian "Cannonball"
　　　　　Adderley Collection..............................$19.95
00673237 Michael Brecker $19.95
00672429 Michael Brecker Collection $22.99
00672315 Benny Carter Plays Standards $22.95
00672394 James Carter Collection........................$19.95
00672349 John Coltrane Plays Giant Steps $19.95
00672529 John Coltrane – Giant Steps.................$17.99
00672494 John Coltrane – A Love Supreme........$15.99
00307393 John Coltrane –
　　　　　Omnibook: C Instruments $24.99
00307391 John Coltrane –
　　　　　Omnibook: B-flat Instruments $27.99
00307392 John Coltrane –
　　　　　Omnibook: E-flat Instruments $29.99
00307394 John Coltrane –
　　　　　Omnibook: Bass Clef Instruments $24.99

00672493 John Coltrane
　　　　　Plays "Coltrane Changes".....................$19.95
00672453 John Coltrane Plays Standards............$22.99
00673233 John Coltrane Solos $22.95
00672328 Paul Desmond Collection......................$19.95
00672379 Eric Dolphy Collection...........................$19.95
00672530 Kenny Garrett Collection $19.95
00699375 Stan Getz $19.99
00672377 Stan Getz – Bossa Novas $22.99
00672375 Stan Getz – Standards $19.99
00673254 Great Tenor Sax Solos $18.99
00672523 Coleman Hawkins Collection $19.99
00673252 Joe Henderson – Selections from
　　　　　"Lush Life" & "So Near So Far"..............$19.95
00673239 Best of Kenny G $19.95
00673229 Kenny G – Breathless $19.95
00672462 Kenny G – Classics in the Key of G $19.95
00672485 Kenny G – Faith: A Holiday Album $15.99
00672373 Kenny G – The Moment $19.95
00672498 Jackie McLean Collection $19.95
00672372 James Moody Collection –
　　　　　Sax and Flute $19.95
00672416 Frank Morgan Collection $19.95
00672539 Gerry Mulligan Collection......................$19.95
00672352 Charlie Parker Collection $19.95
00672561 Best of Sonny Rollins $19.95
00102751 Sonny Rollins
　　　　　with the Modern Jazz Quartet $17.99
00675000 David Sanborn Collection $19.99
00672491 New Best of Wayne Shorter.................$22.99
00672550 The Sonny Stitt Collection....................$19.95
00672524 Lester Young Collection........................$19.99

TROMBONE
00672332 J.J. Johnson Collection $19.99
00672489 Steve Turré Collection $19.99

TRUMPET
00672557 Herb Alpert Collection...........................$17.99
00672480 Louis Armstrong Collection $19.99
00672481 Louis Armstrong Plays Standards........$19.99
00672435 Chet Baker Collection $19.99
00672556 Best of Chris Botti.................................$19.99
00672448 Miles Davis – Originals, Vol. 1 ....$19.95
00672451 Miles Davis – Originals, Vol. 2 ....$19.99
00672450 Miles Davis – Standards, Vol. 1 ....$19.99
00672449 Miles Davis – Standards, Vol. 2 ....$19.95
00672479 Dizzy Gillespie Collection $19.99
00673214 Freddie Hubbard $19.99
00672382 Tom Harrell – Jazz Trumpet $19.95
00672363 Jazz Trumpet Solos................................ $9.95
00672506 Chuck Mangione Collection $19.95
00672525 Arturo Sandoval – Trumpet Evolution....$19.99

HAL•LEONARD®
7777 W. BLUEMOUND RD. P.O. BOX 13819 MILWAUKEE, WI 53213

Visit our web site for a complete listing
of our titles with songlists at
www.halleonard.com

0619
153

Prices, content, and availability subject to change without notice.

The Best-Selling Jazz Book of All Time Is Now Legal!

The Real Books are the most popular jazz books of all time. Since the 1970s, musicians have trusted these volumes to get them through every gig, night after night. The problem is that the books were illegally produced and distributed, without any regard to copyright law, or royalties paid to the composers who created these musical masterpieces.

Hal Leonard is very proud to present the first legitimate and legal editions of these books ever produced. You won't even notice the difference, other than all the notorious errors being fixed: the covers and typeface look the same, the song lists are nearly identical, and the price for our edition is even cheaper than the originals!

Every conscientious musician will appreciate that these books are now produced accurately and ethically, benefitting the songwriters that we owe for some of the greatest tunes of all time!

VOLUME 1
00240221	C Edition	$39.99
00240224	B♭ Edition	$39.99
00240225	E♭ Edition	$39.99
00240226	Bass Clef Edition	$39.99
00286389	F Edition	$39.99
00240292	C Edition 6 x 9	$35.00
00240339	B♭ Edition 6 x 9	$35.00
00147792	Bass Clef Edition 6 x 9	$35.00
00451087	C Edition on CD-ROM	$29.99
00200984	Online Backing Tracks: Selections	$45.00
00110604	Book/USB Flash Drive Backing Tracks Pack	$79.99
00110599	USB Flash Drive Only	$50.00

VOLUME 2
00240222	C Edition	$39.99
00240227	B♭ Edition	$39.99
00240228	E♭ Edition	$39.99
00240229	Bass Clef Edition	$39.99
00240293	C Edition 6 x 9	$35.00
00125900	B♭ Edition 6 x 9	$35.00
00451088	C Edition on CD-ROM	$30.99
00125900	The Real Book – Mini Edition	$35.00
00204126	Backing Tracks on USB Flash Drive	$50.00
00204131	C Edition – USB Flash Drive Pack	$79.99

VOLUME 3
00240233	C Edition	$39.99
00240284	B♭ Edition	$39.99
00240285	E♭ Edition	$39.99
00240286	Bass Clef Edition	$39.99
00240338	C Edition 6 x 9	$35.00
00451089	C Edition on CD-ROM	$29.99

VOLUME 4
00240296	C Edition	$39.99
00103348	B♭ Edition	$39.99
00103349	E♭ Edition	$39.99
00103350	Bass Clef Edition	$39.99

VOLUME 5
00240349	C Edition	$39.99
00175278	B♭ Edition	$39.99
00175279	E♭ Edition	$39.99

VOLUME 6
00240534	C Edition	$39.99
00223637	E♭ Edition	$39.99

Also available:
00154230	The Real Bebop Book	$34.99
00240264	The Real Blues Book	$34.99
00310910	The Real Bluegrass Book	$35.00
00240223	The Real Broadway Book	$35.00
00240440	The Trane Book	$22.99
00125426	The Real Country Book	$39.99
00269721	The Real Miles Davis Book C Edition	$24.99
00269723	The Real Miles Davis Book B♭ Edition	$24.99
00240355	The Real Dixieland Book C Edition	$32.50
00294853	The Real Dixieland Book E♭ Edition	$35.00
00122335	The Real Dixieland Book B♭ Edition	$35.00
00240235	The Duke Ellington Real Book	$22.99
00240268	The Real Jazz Solos Book	$30.00
00240348	The Real Latin Book C Edition	$37.50
00127107	The Real Latin Book B♭ Edition	$35.00
00120809	The Pat Metheny Real Book C Edition	$27.50
00252119	The Pat Metheny Real Book B♭ Edition	$24.99
00240358	The Charlie Parker Real Book C Edition	$19.99
00275997	The Charlie Parker Real Book E♭ Edition	$19.99
00118324	The Real Pop Book – Vol. 1	$35.00
00240331	The Bud Powell Real Book	$19.99
00240437	The Real R&B Book C Edition	$39.99
00276590	The Real R&B Book B♭ Edition	$39.99
00240313	The Real Rock Book	$35.00
00240323	The Real Rock Book – Vol. 2	$35.00
00240359	The Real Tab Book	$32.50
00240317	The Real Worship Book	$29.99

THE REAL CHRISTMAS BOOK
00240306	C Edition	$32.50
00240345	B♭ Edition	$32.50
00240346	E♭ Edition	$35.00
00240347	Bass Clef Edition	$32.50
00240431	A-G CD Backing Tracks	$24.99
00240432	H-M CD Backing Tracks	$24.99
00240433	N-Y CD Backing Tracks	$24.99

THE REAL VOCAL BOOK
00240230	Volume 1 High Voice	$35.00
00240307	Volume 1 Low Voice	$35.00
00240231	Volume 2 High Voice	$35.00
00240308	Volume 2 Low Voice	$35.00
00240391	Volume 3 High Voice	$35.00
00240392	Volume 3 Low Voice	$35.00
00118318	Volume 4 High Voice	$35.00
00118319	Volume 4 Low Voice	$35.00

Complete song lists online at www.halleonard.com

Prices, content, and availability subject to change without notice.

0719
318